William Guy Carr, R.D.

The Conspiracy To Destroy All Existing Governments & Religions

OMNIA VERITAS.

William Guy Carr
(1895-1959)
Commander Royal Canadian Navy

William Guy Carr (1895-1959) was a Canadian naval officer and author. He wrote extensively on conspiracy theories, most notably in his book *Pawns in the Game*. His work has been the subject of both influence and criticism.

THE CONSPIRACY TO DESTROY ALL
EXISTING GOVERNMENTS & RELIGIONS

First published in 1958

Published by
OMNIA VERITAS LTD
OMNIA VERITAS®
www.omnia-veritas.com

Preface

About the Book

Those who find it difficult to accept the fact that the U. S. is the target of political and economic conspiracies are not ready for this book which deals with a conspiracy on a much higher level.

The average man is not acquainted with the history and documentation involved. Also it has not yet been brought home to him that the Powers of Evil are as real as the Powers of Good.

In this book the reader is exposed to Professor Robison's publishing of secret documents and many later disclosures. He is then quickly carried through history by the author who follows the thread of conspiracy through time.

Suddenly the warnings he has heard about one world government become understandable as he learns that the conspiracy has ever aimed to see one government established over the world whose powers they could then usurp. This is quite different from the single government which most Christians are awaiting to be created by the Lord.

The conspirators have a comprehensive philosophy concerning mankind. They are aware that God created this earth and introduced us here through a method of birth which deprived us of personal knowledge of a previous existence. He then endowed us with an intellect which could receive inspiration from both good and evil sources. Thus with a free will bestowed upon him, man was in a position to be tested on this earth as his body put the decisions of his mind into action toward positive or negative goals.

Great care has been taken by the conspirators to ensure that their existence and plans are not revealed through secret oaths, ridicule, and murder. The true doctrine is to be revealed only after their organization has achieved despotic supremacy. Here is revealed a bold and diabolical conspiracy intended to defraud man of his God given freedom through deceit, horror and force.

The masses are to be flattered with whatever lavish praise and extravagant promises will appeal to them with the understanding that, "The opposite of what we promise may be done afterwards ... that is of no consequence."

From the grave Carr's voice speaks,

> "Mail or distribute copies of this issue to everyone you can think of. It is marvelous the results that are obtained when a few copies fall into good hands."

He was ever confident that truth would be victorious.

In 1796 John Robison, Professor of Human Philosophy, and Secretary of the Royal Society, Edinburgh, Scotland, published documents which had been entrusted to his care by members of Weishaupt's Illuminati while he had been touring Europe prior to the outbreak of the French Revolution in 1789. Robison was a high degree Mason. It was for this reason he had been entrusted with the secret documents. He had them in his possession for a considerable time before he read them. When he had finished, he realized they were a copy of Weishaupt's revised version of the Age Old Luciferian conspiracy and an explanation of how he intended to use the members of the Order and Sect of the Illuminati to drive it through to its final goal which is control of the First World Government to be established and the imposition of the Luciferian ideology upon the Human Race by despotic Satanism.

John Robison's publication was entitled *'Proof of a Conspiracy to Destroy all Religions and Governments in Europe.'* The information contained in it simply confirmed what the Bavarian Government had published under the title The Original Writings (Protocols) of the Order and Sect of the Illuminati' in 1786 and what Zwack had also published under the title 'Einige Originalschriften.' The Bavarian Government sent copies of Weishaupt's plan to use his recently organized Illuminati to destroy all existing governments and religions to all the heads of Church and State prior to the outbreak of the French Revolution in 1789. But the warning was ignored. The fact that the Illuminati have had the power to maintain their identity and intention to enslave the Human Race, body, mind, and soul, as a secret has enabled the conspirators to develop the conspiracy to its semi-final stage. The purpose of this article is to tell how the conspiracy was developed since 1798 to the present time. We also expose the details of the blue print drawn up by General Albert Pike, 1850 to 1886, to carry it to its conclusion.

Weishaupt was Professor of Canon Law at Ingolstadt University when he revised, and modernized, the age old Luciferian conspiracy to prevent the Human Race from establishing God's plan for the Rule of Creation upon this earth so that they could ultimately impose the Luciferian ideology upon the Goyim (human cattle) by means of Satanic despotism. From 1770 to 1776 he was financed by the newly organized House of Rothschild in exactly the same way as those who direct the Illuminati's activities today are financed by the Tax-Free Foundations established for that purpose by such multi-millionaires as the Rockefellers, Carnegies and Fords. The Bavarian Government discovered Weishaupt's conspiracy when, in 1786, God struck one of his couriers dead by a stroke of lightning as he rode through Ratisbon on his way to Paris. The police found a copy of the revised version of the conspiracy in transit to members of Weishaupt's Illuminati who had been charged with the responsibility of fomenting the Great French Revolution. This first major project, leading to the ultimate destruction of all governments and religions, was scheduled to break out in 1789.

Weishaupt's plan is extremely simple. He organized the Illuminati and then formed the Grand Orient Lodges to infiltrate the Illuminati into Blue or European Masonry, using the Lodges as their secret headquarters. Thus the conspirators could operate under the cloak of philanthropy.

Weishaupt never intended that any except specially selected Masons, from the Higher Degrees, should learn 'The Full Secret.' Only those known to have defected completely from Almighty God were initiated into the Higher Degrees of the Grand Orient Lodges and told that the Illuminati were a secret organization with the order dedicated to the cause of forming a One World Government—in some form—the powers of which they intended to usurp so they could impose their ideology upon mankind: the worship of Lucifer. Weishaupt stated this action would ensure permanent peace and prosperity. Only initiates into the final degree were permitted to know that the Luciferian Ideology was to be imposed on the Human Race by Satanic despotism.

As will be proved, only the adepts of the Final Degree are initiated as High Priests of the Synagogue of Satan; they worship Lucifer as opposed to our God whom they name Adonay.

The plan the Illuminati put into effect is to use monetary and sex bribery to place influential people under their control. They then use them to further the Illuminati's secret plans. Youths belonging to well-bred families with international leanings are also selected and sent to private schools where Illuminists indoctrinate them with international ideas and then train them so they qualify to fill positions in politics and religion as 'Specialist', 'Experts', and 'Advisors'. The Illuminati then use the wealth, power, and influence of the members to place their 'Agentur' in key positions behind the scenes of all governments' financial, industrial, educational, and religious activity. They then mold policy so that it fits in with the Luciferian plan to promote wars and revolutions on an ever increasing scale. Weishaupt stipulated that the Illuminati should organize, finance, direct, and control Communism,

Naziism, and Political Zionism to facilitate the Illuminati's task of dividing the world's population into opposing camps in ever increasing numbers.

This policy of Self-elimination was to continue until only Communism and Christendom remain as world powers. When this stage of the conspiracy is reached the Illuminati are to provoke the greatest social cataclysm the world has ever known and the Goyim controlled by atheistic communists and those who profess Christianity are to be kept fighting until they have slaughtered each other by the tens of millions. It is during these world wars that the devil reaps his richest harvest in souls.

This wholesale slaughter is to continue, while the Illuminati, their millionaire friends, scientists, and agentur relax in safety and luxury in preestablished self-contained sanctuaries (Southern Florida, the West Indies, and islands of the Caribbean Seas), until both sides have been literally bled white and become absolutely exhausted physically and eco-nomically. They will then have no alternative but to accept a One World Government as their only hope, The Illuminati will then usurp the powers of that government and crown their leader king-despot of the entire world.

Then and not until then, the Synagogue of Satan (who always have and do now control all subversive organizations) will, by universal manifestation make known to the Goyim, for the first time, the true light of the pure doctrine of the Luciferian Doctrine and impose the Luciferian ideology upon what remains of the Human Race by means of Satanic despotism.

Thus we see that the issue is not temporal and materialistic as those who direct the conspiracy would have us believe. We are involved in a continuation of the Luciferian revolt against the supreme power and authority of Almighty God whom the Luciferians name Adonay. We are taught about the infinite goodness of our God but we are kept in ignorance of the fact that the Luciferian revolt started in the celestial world we call Heaven because Lucifer challenged the supremacy of Adonay on the grounds that his plan for the Rule of the Universe was weak and impractical because it was based on the premise that all lesser beings could be educated into knowing Him, loving Him, and serving Him, out of respect for His infinite perfection.

Lucifer claimed that the only way to rule the entire universe is to establish a totalitarian dictatorship, and enforce the Will of the Dictator with absolute despotism. The word Universe as used by those who have accepted the Luciferian ideology in this and other celestial worlds, means The Totality of existing things including the earth, the heavenly or celestial bodies, and all else throughout space.

One cannot understand this all important subject unless he knows the whole truth. We must know the Luciferian ideology as 3 well as the Scriptural history of the struggle which has gone on through the ages of time in this and other worlds between God and Lucifer to decide which plan for the rule of creation will finally be put into effect. Unless we know the whole truth we cannot decide by our God-given gifts of an intellect and free will whether we wish to accept God's plan and love, serve and obey Him for all eternity or literally go to the devil (Lucifer).

The purpose of those who direct the Luciferian conspiracy is to prevent the masses—The Goyim; the Human Cattle— from knowing the whole truth because they know that if we did we would automatically accept God's plan.

The Luciferians therefore rely upon their ability to lie to and deceive those they plan to enslave body, mind, and soul, into believing anything but the truth. That is the reason

Christ referred to the Synagogue of Satan, who direct the Luciferian conspiracy upon this earth as 'Sons of the Devil, whose lusts ye shall do. He was a murderer from the beginning. He knows not the truth because the truth is not in Him.' We must also remember that the words 'Synagogue of Satan' do not, repeat not, mean the Jews because Christ also made it perfectly clear that the Synagogue of Satan 'Are those who call themselves Jews, but are not, and do lie.' The Synagogue of Satan is composed of men and women of many nationalities which have their origin in Cain, Eve's son. My knowledge of the Luciferian Creed has been acquired by reading all the literature I could obtain dealing with the subject and by reading and studying translations of the writings of his Eminence Caro y Rodriguez, Cardinal of Santiago, Chile. I pass on that knowledge in order that you may decide the issue one way or the other.

The Luciferian Creed teaches that Lucifer was the brightest and most intelligent of the Heavenly host. His power and influence were so great that when he challenged the power and supremacy of God (Adonay) he caused a vast number of higher ranks of celestial beings to defect from God and join him. Among these was Satan, the eldest son of Adonay. According to the Luciferian belief, St. Michael, the Archangel, is Satan's brother, and the younger son of Adonay. The Luciferian teachings admit that St. Michael defeated those who had espoused the Luciferian Cause in Heaven. This started the eternal enmity between Satan and St. Michael. According to the Luciferian teaching, 'Hell' is the word used to designate the celestial world to which God banished Lucifer and the more intelligent of the celestial beings who had followed him of their own free will. According to the Luciferian Creed, God (Adonay) decided to give those creatures He considered had been deceived into joining the Luciferian revolt, another chance.

He therefore created other worlds including this earth and inhabited them with the less guilty who had defected from Him in heaven at the time of the revolt. He made them in His own image and like-ness inasmuch as they were bodies infused with the spiritual light of sanctifying grace. In appearance they looked the same as Christ when he permitted Peter, James and John to see him transfigured. God introduced these fallen angels to the new worlds by a method of birth which deprived them of personal knowledge of their previous existence. He endowed them, however, with an intellect, and gave them the use of a free will. Their minds were so constructed that they could receive inspirations from the celestial world both from those who remained faithful to God and those who had joined the Luciferian Cause. Those on trial are intended to sort out these inspirations by using their intellect. The body puts the decisions of the mind into action. All bodily actions must be either positive or negative. Every bodily action is recorded in 'The Book of Life.' The individual thus decides his eternal future; by his bodily actions he proves if he has accepted God's plan for the Rule of the Universe or Lucifer's plan. The results are either 'Good' or 'Evil'.

According to the Luciferian Creed, Lucifer made Satan 'Prince of this world' at the time of its creation. His task was to cause our first parents to defect from God (Adonay), and to prevent their progeny from establishing His plan for the Rule of Creation upon this earth. This creed also teaches that God walked in the Garden of Eden (Paradise) without parents instructing them regarding His plan and His way of life.

Up to this point there appears no great difference between the teachings of the Luciferian Creed and the Holy Scriptures; the difference begins to appear from the time Satan arrived on the scene.

The Luciferian Creed teaches (to the initiates of the lower degrees of the New Palladian Rites, as organized by Albert Pike—of which more later) that God (Adonay) is a jealous and selfish God; He withheld from our first parents knowledge of the pleasures of sexual intercourse—the secret of procreation—because He wished to reserve these pleasures for Himself. This is of course the lie.

God simply postponed making His will regarding procreation known to our first parents until He had thoroughly tested their honesty, integrity and obedience, to make sure they were reliable enough to be entrusted with the secret, and worthy enough to perform that holy and sacred function which would give others a chance to accept God's plan for the rule of creation. Those initiated into the New Palladian Rite are told that Satan bestowed the greatest possible benefaction upon the human race when he initiated Eve into the pleasures of sexual intercourse, thus making known to her the secret of procreation. The Holy Scriptures tell us that Satan caused her to disobey God ('Of the tree of knowledge thou shall not eat.') by promising her that if she accepted his advances, both she and Adam would be made equal in power to God and never know death. In other words, Satan introduced Eve to the Luciferian ideology regarding sex and sexual relations (carnal knowledge) which are diametrically opposed to God's intentions; the act of procreation was to be performed by one man and one woman united for life in the bonds of matrimony. The ritual was to be performed in strict privacy; the love-play was to be based on mutual expressions of joy, appreciation, devotion and gratitude each showed for the other. The climax was to be reached by the spiritual desire of both parties to promote God's plan for the habitation of the world by creating another being who would grow up to love, honour and obey God so as to live happily with Him forever.

Satan's conquest of Eve was an entirely different matter, as it is re-enacted in the ritual of the Adonaicide Mass (Black Mass). According to the ritual in this Mass, Satan's love-play was calculated to arouse the animal passions in Eve to the point when the gratification of the sexual urge over-came all other considerations. He taught her to be voluptuous instead of modest and restrained; to be promiscuous instead of constant to her spouse; to engage in exhibitionism instead of observing strict privacy; to enter into perversions and indulge in excesses instead of moderation. According to Satanism it is perfectly normal to use any medium to gratify the sexual urge, regardless whether it be animal or human. The Babylonian Talmud, (based on the Cabalistic teachings of the promoters of the Luciferian conspiracy), teaches it is perfectly proper for a man to use children as young as three years of age to satisfy his diabolical animal passions. The Luciferian Creed claims Cain was born as the result of the union between Satan and Eve.

Knowing these horrors regarding sex are according to the Luciferian ideology, we can recognize the Satanic influence which inspires such ideas. But it is hard to understand how ministers of Christian denominations can expound the following theories regarding the marriage act.

Recently we read in Church publications, which voice the opinions of the leaders of two different denominations, that it is perfectly right and proper for a married couple to engage in sexual intercourse anywhere convenient; at any time (including the menstrual period) and in any position, providing the act terminates in the way which permits of conception. After reading this abominable advice we concluded the authors had undoubtedly kept their vows of celibacy! There is a vast difference between sexual indulgence for the sake of merely gratifying the animal passions and the holy sacred relationship entered into by a man with his wife who is, and remains, pure in body, mind and soul.

Gratifying animal passion is gross, aggressive, often perverted and sadistic. The act of love and affection performed between a man and his wife in love with one another is a holy and sacred ritual which is truly termed 'A Sacrament'.

Under the influence of the Illuminati's propaganda far too many individuals have entered the marriage contract for the purpose of legalizing sexual relations. Many marriages are nothing but legalized prostitution; still more marriages are marriages of convenience. It is any wonder then, that we humans are born with the stain of Original Sin? We are conceived in sin because the act of procreation is not in accordance with the will of God, but in keeping with the perversions introduced by Satan when he seduced Eve. God in His anger with our first parents withdrew the light of sanctifying grace from their bodies; because of their sin they were reduced from the status of immortals to mortals and were condemned to suffer privations, physical suffering, sickness and death. But God, in His mercy and goodness, through His beloved son, Jesus Christ, gave us another chance to reject the Luciferian ideology as taught by Satanists, and accept His plan for the rule of creation.

If what we explain is not the truth, then why does the Roman Catholic Church put such great importance on the dogma of the Immaculate conception of Mary the mother of Jesus Christ? The Roman Catholic Faith requires all its members to believe that Mary is the only human being born without the stain of original sin because she conceived of the Holy Ghost in accordance with God's plan for the process of procreation.

If Satan hadn't used a perverted version of the sexual relationship to wean Adam and Eve away from God, then why is it that the Skoptsi have practiced self-emasculation since before the advent of Christ, and still emasculate themselves, in order to prove that they reject sex as introduced to the human race in its perverted form by Satan. The Skoptsi believe that only by emasculating themselves can they devote themselves one hundred percent to the service of Almighty God and the establishing of His plan for the rule of creation upon this earth.

The Skoptsi scoff at ministers and priests of the Christian religion who are afraid to emasculate themselves so they can render perfect service to Almighty God. Christ's apostles were often asked by those who wished to become their disciples if self-emasculation was mandatory. St. Matthew deals with this very delicate question in Chapter 10:7-12. Verse 12 reads 'For there are eunuchs which were made eunuchs of men; and there be eunuchs which have made themselves eunuchs for the Kingdom of Heaven's sake. *He who is able to receive it let him receive it.*'[1]

Dealing with this same subject St. Paul told his followers that it is better for human beings to renounce sexual relationship, as based on the perverted version of sexual relationship, separates many human beings from Almighty God that caused Thessalonians 4:1-7 to be written into the Holy Scriptures 'Brethren, even as you have learned from us how you ought to walk, and to please God—as indeed you are walking—we beseech and exhort you, in the Lord Jesus, to make even greater progress. For you know what

---

[1] Note: Ref. is to 'this extraordinary sacrifice.' - Ed.

precepts I have given to you by the Lord Jesus. For this is the will of God; your sanctification; that you abstain from immorality; that everyone of you learn how to possess his vessel in holiness and honor, not in the passion of lust like the gentiles (Luciferians or Satanists) who do not know God—for God has not called us into uncleanness, but unto holiness in Christ Jesus our Lord.'

It is on this premise that St. Augustine bases his opinion that it was the perversion of the sexual relationship, as intended by Almighty God, coupled with disobedience by Adam and Eve to His law and revealed plan for the rule of Creation, aggravated by a display of lack of Faith in His perfections and infinite goodness which constitutes Original Sin.

Once this great truth is accepted and understood it is a simple matter to understand how the continuing Luciferian conspiracy has been developed on this earth, for the purpose of enslaving the survivors of the Human Race, body, mind and soul. (It also explains the current flood of sex appeal by radio, TV; pornographic pictures; lewd displays of the female figure; sexy song—Presley rhythm—rock and roll).

Voltaire wrote that; In order to lead the masses into new subjection the Illuminati must lie to them like the Devil himself, not timidly or for a time only, but boldly and always. He told his fellow Illuminists: 'We must make them lavish promises and use extravagant phrases ... The opposite of what we promise may be done afterwards ... that is of no consequence.'

It is on the premise that a human being can't indulge his sexual desires, and serve God efficiently, that causes the Roman Catholic Church to require those who seek Holy Orders to take the vow of chastity and celibacy. But most revealing of all is the fact that the knowledge of the terrible and tremendous influence sex, as taught by Satanism, has over the lives of its adepts, that some men who have been admitted as High Priests of the Luciferian Creed have emasculated themselves, or ordered their doctors to emasculate them, to prevent sexual considerations interfering with their determination to establish the Luciferian totalitarian dictatorship upon this earth. According to reliable sources of information Kadar is one such person.

One of America's leading magazines, late in 1956, published the story of how Kadar took over in Hungary and put an end to the abortive uprising. The author claimed Kadar had been emasculated by his enemies while in their custody. That statement is a lie. Kadar was castrated by his own physician at his own request. He wished to become a perfect adept of the Luciferian Cause.

Kadar is such a fanatic that, after he had sup-pressed the Hungarian revolt, he ordered 45,000 Hungarian youths, who had been taken prisoners, to be emasculated. He then sent them to special camps where they have been trained to become Agentur of the Illuminati to be used to develop the Luciferian conspiracy in its final-phase. This is all very horrible, but true. N.B.N. stated in 1956 that the Hungarian revolt had been organized by the Illuminati outside Hungary and that its purpose was to test out in actual practice the feasibility of Pike's plan to provoke the final social cataclysm between people controlled by Atheistic-Communists, and those who profess Christianity. Evidence since received proves we were absolutely correct in our contentions.

The Luciferian Creed teaches that the Luciferian conspiracy advanced at such a pace that God decided to send St. Michael on earth, in the form of Jesus Christ, to halt the conspiracy and rout those who comprised the Synagogue of

Satan; it also teaches that St. Michael (Christ) failed in His mission. Pike built up the ceremonial of the Adonaicide Mass around the seduction of Eve by Satan, the Luciferian's victory over Christ, and His death at the instigation of the Illuminati.

Christ did come to redeem us by setting us free from the bonds of Satan with which we are bound. He told us Satan had obtained control over all those in high places in government, religion, the sciences and social services. His birth in a stable proves to us that if we wish to establish God's plan for the rule of Creation upon this earth, we must start at the bottom to educate the majority of mankind. Christ made it abundantly clear that it was hopeless, and useless, to even try to start at the top. Acceptance of this lesson will create a spiritual revolution'.

Christ also told us that there is only one way to end the Luciferian conspiracy and that is to teach the whole truth concerning it to the people of all nations. He assured us that if we made the truth generally known, and explained to the masses that the Luciferian ideology requires their absolute enslavement, body, mind, and soul, the reaction would be such that public opinion would become a greater force than they could control. Weishaupt and Pike both admit this truth. They insist that any Illuminist executive so much as suspected of defecting must be executed as a traitor. Weishaupt and Pike both admit this truth. They insist that defecting must be executed as a traitor. Weishaupt wrote that if one man was allowed to divulge their secret, their plans could be set back three thousand years or ended completely. This is very consoling information. It is to carry out this mandate as given to us by Christ that we tell how Weishaupt used Thomas Jefferson to transfer the revised version of the Luciferian conspiracy to America.

Jefferson was among the financiers, politicians, economists, scientists, industrialists, professional men, and religious leaders who had accepted the idea that a One World Government directed by men of brains (Illuminists) was the only way to end wars and revolutions. Jefferson was so high in the executive councils of the Illuminati that he secretly had their insignia inscribed upon the back of the Great Seal of America in readiness for the day they would take over the government. This information will shock a great number of American citizens, so we will quote authentic documents and historical events, knowledge of which has been carefully withheld from the general public in Canada and the U.S.A.

1789, John Robison, himself a high Mason, confirmed that the Illuminati had infiltrated into American Masonic lodges.

July 19th, 1798, David A. Pappan, President of Harvard University, warned the graduating class regarding the influence Illuminism was having on American politics and religion. (We wonder what he would have to say about Harvard itself if he were alive today!)

Thanksgiving Day 1789, Jedediak Morse preached against Illuminism. He warned his congregation, and the people of the United States, that the Illuminists cover their true purpose by infiltrating into Masonic lodges and hiding their subversive acts and intentions under the cloak of philanthropy.

1799, John Cosens Ogden exposed the fact that Illuminists in New England were indefatigably engaged in destroying religion and government in America under feigned regard for their safety.

1800, John Quincy Adams opposed Jefferson for the Presidency of the United States. Adams had organized the New England Masonic Lodges. He wrote three letters to Col. Wm. L. Stone exposing Jefferson's subversive activities. The information contained in these letters is credited with enabling Adams to win the election. The letters referred to are (or were) on exhibition in the Rittenhouse Sq. Library, Philadelphia.

1800, Captain Wm. Morgan took upon himself the duty of informing other Masons how and why the Illuminati were using their lodges for subversive purposes. The Illuminati delegated one of their members, Richard Howard, to execute Morgan as a traitor. Morgan tried to escape to Canada. He failed.

Avery Allyn made an affidavit and swore that he had heard Richard Howard report to a meeting of Knights Templars in St. John's Hall, New York, how he had completed his mission to 'execute' Morgan successfully. Arrangements had then been made to ship Howard back to Liverpool, England. Masonic records prove that as the result of this incident thousands of Masons seceded from the Northern Jurisdiction.

1829, an English Illuminist named 'Fanni' Wright lectured to a carefully selected group of Illuminists in the new Masonic Temple in New York. She explained the Luciferian ideology regarding 'free love' and 'sexual liberty'. She also informed the American Illuminists it was intended to organize, and finance, Atheistic-Communism for the purpose of furthering their own secret plans and ambitions. Among those who helped put this phase of the Luciferian conspiracy into effect were Clinton Roosevelt, (a direct ancestor of F.D. Roosevelt), Horace Greeley, and Charles Dada.

1834, to cover up their real purpose, the above named organized the Loco-Foco Party.

1835, they changed the name to The Whig Party', and used it to raise the funds used to finance Mordecai Mark Levi (Karl Marx) while he wrote The Communist Manifesto' and 'Das Kapital' in Soho, London, England. Both these publications were written under direct supervision of the Illuminati. They were designed to enable the Illuminati to organize Atheistic-Communism as required by Adam Weishaupt's plan completed in 1776.

1834, the Illuminati appointed Giuseppe Mazzini their 'Director of Political Action'. This title was a cover-up for the office of 'Director of Revolutionary Activities,' Leon de Poncins on page 65 confirms what I had published in this regard in 'Pawns In the Game' and 'Red Fog Over America', i.e., that Mazzini was in close contact with, and directed the revolutionary activities of leaders located throughout the entire world. Mazzini met General Albert Pike shortly after President Jefferson Davis had disbanded his Indian Auxiliary Troops on account of atrocities they had committed under the cloak of war. Pike was totalitarian minded and readily agreed to join the Illuminati.

1850, at the age of 41, Albert Pike infiltrated into Freemasonry and was initiated into the Western Star Lodge in Little Rock, Ark. Backed by the Illuminati, his rise within masonry was phenomenal.

1859, on January 2nd., Pike was elected Sovereign Grand Commander of the Supreme Council of the Southern Jurisdiction of the U.S.A. He came in close contact with an adept of the Luciferian Creed named Moses Holbrook who was Sovereign Commander of the Supreme Council of Charleston, S.C. Together they worked out the ritual for a modernized version of the Luciferian 'Black Mass' which is based in Cabalistic teachings. Then Holbrook died and Pike introduced the 'Adonaicide Mass' to be used by those who had been admitted into the full secret and the final degree of the New Palladian Rites.

The ritual of the 'Adonaicide Mass' requires the celebrant to initiate the Priestess who plays the part of Eve, in the pleasures of sex as taught to Eve by Satan. Thus Satan's victory over Eve is perpetuated, and those present are reminded how sex is still used to cause those they wish to control to defect from God also.

The ritual also requires the immolation of a victim-human, animal, or fowl. This sacrifice is offered to Lucifer to commemorate the Synagogue of Satan's victory over Christ. The blood of the victim is passed around and sipped by those present, then parts of the flesh are eaten. This is done to ridicule Christ for telling us that 'He who eateth my flesh and drinketh my blood will have eternal life.' Note: Chicago police are still investigating three such ritual murders.

The celebrant also desecrates and defiles a Host consecrated by a priest of the Roman Catholic Church. This act is performed to prove to those present that God (Adonay) is not supreme. It also indicates the determination of those present to destroy all other religions. Note: Just recently agentur of the Illuminati stole the tabernacle out of a Roman Catholic Church in New Jersey to obtain consecrated Hosts.

All Adonaicide Masses terminate in an orgy of eating, drinking, and sexual indulgences. Pike ruled, 'That in order for an adept of the highest degrees to be in complete control of his passions, which lead so many hearts astray, thou must use women often and without passion; thou wilt thus become master of thy desires, and thou wilt enchain women.' Pike also wrote 'The Lodges of Brothers which fail to annex a lodge of sisters for the common use is incomplete.' See page 578 of *'La Femme et L'enfant dans la Franc-Maconnerie Universelles.'* by A.C. De La Rive, which deals specifically with Lodges of Adoption which are used to introduce women into Palladian rites. Note: Wilma Montesi died after being used as a priestess at an Adonaicide Mass. She had taken part in a sexual marathon. She died of an overdose of drugs, administered to stimulate the sexual appetite, and from physical exhaustion. Her body was found on a beach near Naples in Italy. The scandal involved High Officials of both Church and State in Italy.

Because of his diligence in the Luciferian Cause, Pike was elected Sovereign Pontiff of Universal Freemasonry. As such he was assisted by ten Ancients of the Supreme Lodge of the Grand Orient of Charleston, S.C. Working in the mansion he built in Little Rock, Ark., in 1840, he drew up the blue-print for the final stages of the Luciferian conspiracy. As we will prove later, the final social cataclysm is to be between the masses controlled by Atheistic- Communists and the masses which adhere to the Christian religion. It is this diabolical plan which justifies the definition of the word 'Goyim' to mean 'human cattle being prepared for the slaughter.'

In order to put this diabolically inspired plot into effect, Pike organized the New Palladian Rites. He ordered Mazzini to establish supreme councils in Rome and Berlin to work in cooperation with the headquarters he had established in Charleston, S.C. The Supreme Council in Rome was to direct 'Political Action'; the one in Berlin was to be the Dogmatic Directory. The three supreme councils were to direct the subversive activities of the 23 other councils Pike organized in strategic locations in North America, South America, Europe, Asia, Africa, and Oceania. Note: It was executive members of these councils who flew to Georgia to attend the secret meeting held in the King & Prince Hotel on St. Simon's Island, Feb. 14th., to 17th., 1957, as reported in the May issue of N.B.N.

To prove that the 'Full Secret' is only made known to those who qualify for initiation in the final degree of the Palladian Rite, which makes them members of The Great White Lodge', and High Priests of the Luciferian Creed, we will quote a letter written by Mazzini to Dr. Breidenstine before he was made an adept of the final rite. He wrote:

> 'We form an association of brothers in all points of the globe. We wish to break every yoke. Yet there is one that is unseen; that can be hardly felt, yet that weighs on us. Whence comes it? Where is it? No one knows, or at least no one tells. This association is secret even to us, the veterans of secret societies.'

In order to be able to provoke the final social cataclysm between Communists and Christians, Pike had to put Illuminists in control of the Vatican's political policies. To enable the Illuminati to infiltrate into the Vatican, Pike ordered Mazzini to build up an anti Vatican atmosphere in Europe until, as we know, the lives of all within the Vatican were threatened. Then Karl Rothschild, the son of Mayer Anselm Rothschild (who financed Weishaupt's organization of the Illuminati) intervened on behalf of the Vatican on the grounds that he wished to prevent unnecessary bloodshed Thus one of the highest members of the Illuminati won the gratitude and appreciation of the Pope and Vatican officials He then placed agentur of the Illuminati within the Vatican as Experts and advisers on finance and politics. Thus they made good Weishaupt's boast when he wrote 'We will infiltrate into that place (The Vatican) and once inside we will never come out. We will bore from within until it remains nothing but an empty shell.'

Since the Illuminati infiltrated into the Vatican those who direct the Luciferian conspiracy have fomented two world wars, which divided Christendom into opposing armies, Christians of all denominations blew each other off the face of this earth by the millions. The net result is that the masses controlled by Atheistic Communism are now equal in strength to what remains of Christendom. What has happened to date is strictly in accordance with Weishaupt's revision of the Luciferian conspiracy. How it has happened is strictly in keeping with the blue print of action drawn up by Albert Pike, 1850 to 1886, in his mansion in Little Rock, Ark. The Secret Archives of the Vatican are more complete than any other in this world. What a difference there would have been in the pages of history if the Illuminati had not had the power to impose a conspiracy of silence upon all governments, political and religious.

I have many letters from Priests who have lived in Rome, and studied in the Vatican. They give a wealth of evidence to prove that the Holy Father is little better than a prisoner within the Vatican exactly in the same way that the President of the United States is a prisoner within the White House, the Queen of England a prisoner in Buckingham Palace, and Khrushchev a prisoner with in the Kremlin. Only once, in recent years, has the constant surveillance maintained over the Pope been relaxed. That was when his Holiness was thought to be a death's door. We are told he had sunk so low that only a modern miracle could have given him the strength to summon an official he knew he could trust. He ordered this official to send out an appeal and ask all Roman Catholics 'To pray for the silent Church.'

Pike restricted initiation into the New Palladian Rite to men and women who had been proved to have defected from God and sold their souls to Satan in return for material success and carnal pleasures. But such is the cunning, and guile, of those who control the Synagogue of Satan that not even members of the New Palladian Rite are admitted to the full secret until they have been tested further. The manner in which 'The Great White Lodge' (The High Priests of the Luciferian Creed) maintain their secret was fully illustrated when another Act of God caused top secret documents, issued by Pike, to fall into hands other than intended. Mazzini died in 1872. Pike picked Adriano Lemmi to succeed him as Director of Political Action. Lemmi had been initiated in the New Palladian Rite. He was a worshiper of Satan.

Pike instructed him in the full secret. He explained that Lucifer is the only god other than Adonay, and that the ultimate purpose of the continuing conspiracy is to impose the Luciferian ideology upon man kind.

The facts surrounding this incident were disclosed by Margiotta's book 'Adriano Lemmi Chef Supreme des Franc Masons.' The fact that only the few initiated in the Highest degree of the Palladian Rites are in possession of the full secret was proved again when Pike found it necessary to issue the following letter of instruction to those Illuminists he had selected to direct the activities of the 23 councils he had established throughout the world. A copy of this letter dated July 14, 1889, also got astray. It is quoted by A.C. De La Rive on page 587 of 'La Femme et L'enfant dans la Franc-Maçonnerie Universelles.'

We quote,

> 'That which we must say to the crowd is 'We worship God', but it is the God that one adores without superstition .. The Masonic religion should be, by all of us initiates of the high degrees, maintained in the purity of the Luciferian doctrine .. If Lucifer were not God, would Adonay, whose deeds prove his cruelty, perfidy and hatred of men,

barbarism and repulsion for science, would Adonay, and his priests, calumniate him? Yes! Lucifer is God. And unfortunately Adonay is also God. For the Eternal law is that there is no light without shade, no beauty without ugliness, no white without black, for the absolute can only exist as two Gods. Thus the doctrine of Satanism is a heresy, and the true, and pure, philosophical religion is the belief in Lucifer, the equal of Adonay, but Lucifer God of light and God of Good, is struggling for humanity against Adonay the God of darkness and evil.'

History proves that since 1776 the conspiracy has been developed exactly as Weishaupt intended simply because those who direct it have been able to maintain secrecy regarding their ultimate intention to enslave what remains of the human race-body, mind, and soul. We will now reveal the plans the Illuminati intend to follow from now to the end.

Both Weishaupt and Pike required that Political Zionism be organized, financed, and controlled by the Illuminati so that it could be used first to create a sovereign state in which they, the Illuminati, would crown their leader King-despot of the entire universe, and secondly to enable the Illuminati to foment World War Three. Political Zionism was organized by Herzl, 1897. Can any person, still able to exercise his God-given intellect, deny that this part of the plot isn't being developed right now in the Near and Middle East? If we permit World War Three to break out, Zionism and the Moslem world will be wiped out, and the remaining nations eliminated as world powers, then only Atheistic-Communism and Christianity will remain standing between the Illuminati and their goal.

In a letter Pike wrote to Mazzini Aug. 15, 1871, he explains what is to happen when World War Three has ended. (A copy of this letter is, or was, in the Library of the British Imperial Museum, London, England.)

> 'We (the Illuminati) shall unleash the Nihilists and the Atheists, and we shall provoke a formidable social cataclysm which in all its horror will show clearly to the nations the effects of absolute atheism, origin of savagery and of the most bloody turmoil. Then everywhere, the citizens obliged to defend themselves against the world minority, or revolutionaries, will exterminate those destroyers of civilization, and the multitude, disillusioned with Christianity, whose deistic spirits will be from that moment without compass (direction) anxious for an ideal, but without knowing where to render its adoration, will receive the true light, through the universal manifestation of the pure doctrine of Lucifer, brought finally out in the public view, a manifestation which will result from the general reactionary movement which will follow the destruction of Christianity and Atheism, both conquered and exterminated at the same time.'

If any person still doubts the truth let me tell that person that His Eminence Cardinal y Rodriguez of Chile tried to warn both Catholics and Masons of their impending fate in 1925.

When F.D. Roosevelt was elected President of the U.S.A. he was so sure the conspiracy would reach its final goal during his lifetime that in 1933 he had the Illuminati's insignia, (which Jefferson secretly had embossed on the back of the American Great Seal) printed on the back of American dollar bills. This was to notify Illuminists throughout the world that the Illuminati were now in absolute control of American finance, politics, and the social sciences. Roosevelt called this 'The New Deal'.

Roosevelt's foreign policy built up Atheistic-Communism until it was equal in strength in every way to that of Christendom. He was so confident that he would be the first

King-despot that he had the audacity in 1942 to tell Winston Churchill, 'The time has come when the British Empire must be dis-solved in the interests of world peace.' This incident took place in Vallentia Harbout, Newfoundland, when they first met to discuss NATO. To what kind of peace did Roosevelt refer? Peace under a Luciferian dictatorship is what he meant!

We will now show how the Illuminati infiltrated into the British Royal Household. Since 1942 Adm. Louis Mountbatten has been the 'Power behind the throne' in Britain. Under his influence and direction, India and several other parts of the British Empire have 'gained their independence.' This is a polite way of saying they have seceded from the British Crown. What the public thought was wish-ful thinking on Roosevelt's part is rapidly becoming an accomplished fact. Roosevelt knew what the Illuminati had planned. His slip of the tongue when talking to Churchill proves the truth of the old saying, 'When drink is in, the truth will out.' The fact remains that the British Empire, in less than fifty years, has been reduced from the greatest power on earth to a third class power. Britain's Queen is married to Admiral Mountbatten's nephew. Philip was 'Adopted' by the Admiral when a young boy.

Everyone knows that Prince Philip has extremely liberal views and opinions. Very few know that he was privately educated, at his uncle's instigation, at Gordonstoun, Scotland, by Dr. Kurt Hahn, an Illuminist Hitler kicked out of Germany.

Dr. Kurt Hahn is unquestionably an agentur of the Illuminati. In Germany he served on the Executive Committee of the Communist Party but he is not an atheist. He directed the Communist policy in Germany so that it enabled the Illuminati to foment World War Two. Take him any way you wish, the fact remains, he is a fully informed, highly trained, and experienced subversive.

Gordonstoun School is only one of three he has established in accordance with Weishaupt's plan for the Illuminati to indoctrinate and train youths of well-bred families with international leanings to be agentur of the Illuminati. The other two schools Dr. Kurt Hahn established are located in Salem, Germany, and Anavryta, Greece.

We want to make it absolutely clear the N.B.N. does not, repeat not say that youths so trained realize the purpose for which they are being trained. E.H. Norman was one youth so tramed. He came to a very sticky end. So do many of the others. They are just Pawns In The Game.

Queen Elizabeth II is also Head of the Protestant Church in England. Obviously because of forces beyond her control, Canon C.E. Raven has been appointed spiritual 'adviser' to the Royal Household. The Canon has been married three times. His third wife professed to be an Atheist.

She was publicized as 'A heroine of the French Resistance Movement.' One thing is certain, since this appointment was made Her Majesty has never made reference to God Almighty in her Christmas messages to her people. But most significantly, in her last address, she used the jargon of the Illuminati and said, 'The chain reaction of the Powers of Light, to illuminate the new age (New Order) ahead of us.'

Such is the power of those who direct the Illuminati that they instructed another of their agentur (also named Hahn) to celebrate Elizabeth's accession to the throne by having this German born Canadian artist alter the photo Her Majesty had approved to be used on Canadian Bank Notes.

Hahn cleverly concealed the face of Satan in the hair do of the Queen. In Illuminist symbolism this meant, "We now have 'the ear of the Queen' Our agentur are so close to her person She doesn't even suspect their presence." N.B.N brought this outrage to the attention of the Canadian House of Commons, through Mr John Blackmore, P.M., and as the result new plates were made and new bank notes issued. We have tried to inform the Queen's husband of the true purpose of the Illuminati but so far without success.

Since Roosevelt died, American Foreign Policy and that of the UNO has been decided by the Illuminists on the Council of Foreign Relations who occupy the Harold Pratt Building in New York. This headquarters of international intrigue was provided, and is financed, by the Rockefellers, Ford, and Carnegie Tax free foundations. Since the turn of the century the Rockefellers have taken over direction of the continuing conspiracy from the Rothschilds. The foreign policy has been to contain Communism, not to destroy it. International Communism has to be kept equal in strength to the whole of Christendom, otherwise Pike's diabolical plan for the final social cataclysm cannot be put into effect. It is this policy which explains why MacArthur wasn't allowed to destroy Communism during the Korean War. It was this policy that caused the UNO to demand that Britain and France withdraw their troops when they landed in Suez with the firm intention of putting an end to Nasser's subversive activities in Egypt and the Middle East. When MacArthur persisted in his intention to destroy Communism he was fired.

When Anthony Eden sent troops into Egypt he also was fired. For What? Insubordination to those who direct the Illuminati?

Since Jefferson's time the citizens of the U S A have gradually been conditioned for the day when the Illuminati decide to take over. Exactly the same thing has been going on in Canada. We will know the hour for subjugation has arrived when the President of the U S A and the Prime Minister in Canada, declare a State of Emergency and set up a military dictatorship on the pretense that such action is necessary to protect the people from Communist aggression. The Communist Parties, in both our countries are being 'contained because the Illuminati intend to use them to bring about 'The State of Emergency.' The F.B.I. and the R.C.M.P. could, in 48 hours, clean out every Communist, and every other kind and type of subversive if permitted to do so. The heads of the F.B.I. and the R.C.M.P. know who are the secret Powers. Only the general support of the public will free them from the chains with which they, like the rest of us, are bound.

When the Communists are ordered to revolt they will be allowed to run wild as they were in Russia until they have murder ed everybody whose names are on the Illuminati's liquidation lists. Then the agentur of the Illuminati will appear upon the scene and take over control under the pretense they are the saviours of the people. Lenin boasted that 'When the time arrives the United States will fall into our (The Illuminati's) hands like over ripe fruit.' The plan by which the Illuminati intend to take over from the Communists is completed.

The personnel have been selected to carry out the details of the plan. They are being trained in the building in Chicago known as 'Thirteen Thirteen', East 60th Street. It is located on property belonging to the University of Chicago. This Illuminist training center is financed by the same foundations that finance the Council of Foreign Relations in New York. The Illumimsts engaged in this project call themselves 'The Public Administration Services.' They pretend to improve the Civic Governments and Social Services. In reality they train selected agentur to occupy key positions in all levels of civic government.

Graduates of the Public Administration Services have already been placed as 'Specialists', 'Experts', and 'Advisors' by the Illuminati with the following associations:

❖ Am Public Works Assn.

❖ Public Personnel Assn.

❖ Governor's Conference

❖ Municipal Finance Officers Assn.

❖ National Assn Attorneys General

❖ International City Mgrs Assn.

❖ Am. Committee International Municipal Assn.

❖ Am. Municipal Assn.

❖ Conference of Chief Justices

❖ Public Administration Service

❖ National Institute of Municipal Clerks

❖ Nat. Assn. of State Budget Officers

❖ Federation of Tax Administrators

❖ Nat. Assn. of Housing & And Redevelopment

❖ Council of State Governments

❖ Am. Public Welfare Assn.

❖ Interstate Clearing House for Mental Health

❖ Am. Society for Public Administration

❖ Am. Society of Planning Officials

❖ Nat. Assn. of Assessing Officers

❖ Nat. Assn. State Purchasing Officials

❖ Nat. Legislative Conference

The policy of those who direct the Public Administration Services in 'Thirteen—Thirteen' is to get agentur trained under them appointed as City Managers. The City Managers then appoint other graduates of 'Thirteen—Thirteen' as heads of the various civic departments. These in turn bring in others trained in 'Thirteen—Thirteen' until they have control of the municipal government at the top. They pretend they work in the interests of efficiency. What they do in actual fact is usurp the powers of the electorate. Dade County and Miami, and Chicago are already controlled by graduates from 'Thirteen—Thirteen'. In the case of Miami it was necessary that this control should be established immediately. Southern Florida is one of the sanctuaries of the Illuminati and they must be in a position to bring their friends into that sanctuary and exclude from it those for whom they have no use if, and when, a state of emergency is declared. Illuminists in Chicago and Miami control the civic administration, not the people.

Within the walls of 'Thirteen—Thirteen', agentur of the Illuminati are being trained how they are to take over municipal governments, and state parliaments, and subjugate the Goyim (human cattle) when ordered to do so. They are told how they must first of all represent themselves as 'The Saviours of the people', sent to save the masses from further persecutions at the hands of the Communists. They are taught how to lead the masses from Communist oppression and place them under new subjection by the Illuminati. That, ladies and gentlemen, is the setup. If you wish to become better informed about 'Thirteen—Thirteen' send for 'Closer-Up', c/o Time for Truth Press, P.O. Box 2223, Palm Beach, U.S.A.

Our purpose in writing this article is to prove that the Illuminati was organized by Weishaupt to direct the Luciferian conspiracy to its final goal; to prove that the Illuminati is controlled at the top by the Synagogue of Satan. The S.O.S. in turn is controlled by the few who are, in actual fact, the High Priests of the Luciferian Creed also known as the 'Great White Lodge.' We have also tried to prove that the hidden purpose of the Luciferian hierarchy is to prevent us establishing God's plan for the rule of creation upon this earth in order to prevent God's will being done here as it is in heaven. Their objective is to impose the Luciferian ideology upon mankind and enforce their edicts by Satanic despotism. For purposes of deception they refer to the Luciferian Totalitarian dictatorship as The New Order'.

The Luciferian ideology requires The New Order' shall consist of two classes—Governors and slaves. The Ruler and his governors will consist of the High Priests of the Luciferian Creed, their Illuminati and top-level agentur, a few millionaires, scientists, economists, and professional men who have proved themselves devoted to the Luciferian

Cause, with sufficient police and soldiers to enforce obedience upon the Goyim.

All other human beings are to be reduced to one common level by interbreeding white, blacks, yellows, and reds. The mongrelization of the human race is to be speedily accomplished by artificial insemination. Women will be scientifically selected and used as human incubators. They will be made pregnant with semen taken from specially selected males. The birth rate will be strictly limited to the requirements of the state. As it is written in the Illuminati's diabolical plan, 'After we obtain control the very name of God will be erased from the lexicon of life.' In the jargon of the Illuminati this means that scientifically applied psychopolitics (brain washing) will be used to obliterate from the minds of the human slaves all knowledge of Almighty God (Adonay). The Illuminists intend to make Zombies of all those for whom they do not have some special use.

Let me issue this final warning. Wars (regardless of whether they be called aggressive or preventive wars), revolutions (regardless of whether or not they be called counter-revolutions), racial intolerance, religious intolerance, religious bigotry, and persecution and hatred will not provide a solution to our problem. Only by making the whole truth known will we put an end to the Luciferian conspiracy upon this earth. If we continue to keep silence, because of the risks involved, the Luciferian conspiracy will progress to the final social cataclysm when the Goyim, with the use of atomic bombs and nerve gas, will slaughter each other by the tens of millions while the Illuminati, and their friends, bask in luxury on the sunny beaches of their sanctuaries. Those who wish to stand up and be counted as for God and against lucifer don't need arms. They don't need money. All they need is set forth clearly in the Scriptures. Read Ephesians 6:10-17.

> 'Brethren, be strengthened in the Lord, and in His power. Put on the armour of God, that you may be able to stand against the wiles of the devil.
>
> For our wrestling is not against flesh and blood, but against Principalities and the Powers, against the rulers of this darkness, against the spiritual forces of wickedness on high. Therefore, take up the armour of God, that you may resist in the evil day, and stand in all things perfect. Stand therefore, having girded your loins with truth, and having put on the breast-plate of justice, and having your feet shod with the readiness of the gospel of peace, in all things taking up the shield of faith, with which you may be able to quench all the fiery darts of the most wicked one. And take unto you the helmet of salvation and the sword of the spirit, that is, the word of God.'

Could anything be plainer or clearer? The only people we should hate are those of the Synagogue of Satan. They are wolves in sheep's clothing.

Those are the ones Christ hated and exposed. If we break the conspiracy of silence; if we insist that our elected representatives stop playing politics and get to work and establish God's plan for the rule of creation on this earth, then God will intervene on behalf of those who prove they wish to be of His elect. The issue is up to us. It is we who must make the decision. If we sincerely wish to live for all eternity according to God's plan then the only way we can prove our .sincerity is to work to put His plan into operation on this earth. God's plan is detailed in the Holy Scriptures. It isn't in accordance with the United Nations Charter or the ideology expounded by the One Worlders.

Mail or distribute copies of this issue to everyone you can think of. It is marvelous the results that are obtained when a few copies fall into good hands. If you believe what we have explained then it is your duty to pass this knowledge on to as many others as you can contact. Some few will accept the knowledge and truth. Others will reject it. That is not your concern. You will be judged by the effort you put into the work, not by the results you obtain. You don't have to make yourself a pest.

Use patience instead of a club. Use reason instead of abuse. Be kind and considerate Instead of pugnacious and aggressive. Start people thinking and then let them feel they thought the matter out themselves. Those who serve the Illuminati devote every waking hour to further their cause. Can we, if we wish to earn our eternal reward, do less?

We need the cooperation of the Clergy of all religions which teach belief in a God other than Lucifer. We particularly need the active interest of all ministers of the Christian religion. If we can persuade them to lift the lid and break the conspiracy of silence, and tell the whole truth to their congregations, the Illuminati will not be able to proceed with their plan to foment World War Three and the final social cataclysm. The ordained priests of God assume a great responsibility when they accept Holy Orders. Regardless of what the consequences may be they are in duty, and honor, bound to tell the members of their flocks the whole truth. If they don't they leave their charges innocent victims of those who seek possession of their immortal souls.

In conclusion, I ask the 400,000,000 Catholics scattered throughout the world this question. If what I explain in this article is not the truth, why do you recite the following prayer after every low mass? 'Holy St. Michael, Archangel, defend us in the day of battle; be our safeguard against the snares and wickedness of the devil. May God rebuke him, we humbly pray; and do thou, 0 Prince of the Heavenly Host, by the power of God, thrust down to hell Satan, and all wicked spirits, who wander through this world seeking the ruin of souls.'

Either what we tell you regarding the Luciferian conspiracy is the truth or else the words of the above prayer are nonsense. I know Who composed this great prayer. I have told you why he composed it. I feel certain God is ready to heed our prayers just as soon as we prove, by action, we are worthy of His intervention.

Epilogue

About the Author

Commander Carr's last two works are now coming forth posthumously. The first and smallest of these is this work. They deal with the International Conspiracy and are based upon investigations and studies which have taken him into nearly every country in the world.

Carr has had an outstanding naval career. His deep background in history and geopolitics coupled with a penetrating mind made effective his relentless attempt to trace events back to their source and concepts forward to their ultimate conclusion.

The Conspiracy is not for the politically naive (whether the product of formal University training or not). It is for those who are already aware that there is a downward slide of our Western Civilization under a variety of influences which play in concert beyond what could be expected by mere chance.

In writing for such men, Carr displays none of the vindictiveness that characterizes some who profess patriotic leanings. Carr counsels love and patience.

> "You will be judged by the effort you put into the work, not by the results you obtain. You don't have to make yourself a pest. Use patience instead of a club. Use reason instead of abuse. Be kind and considerate instead of

pugnacious and aggressive. Start people thinking and then let them feel that they thought the matter out themselves."

No wonder Carr's books have been so well received. Some have gone through many printings. Though deceased one may easily imagine him as being busily engaged in the cause of truth in his present estate.

Other titles

OMNIA VERITAS | OMNIA VERITAS LTD PRESENTS

THE DISPOSSESSED MAJORITY

THE TRAGIC AND HUMILIATING FATE OF THE AMERICAN MAJORITY

OMNIA VERITAS

Omnia Veritas Ltd presents:

Fatima and the GREAT CONSPIRACY

This meant creating or making money out of nothing, being allowed to call it money, and to lend it to the public at a high interest rate.

This private syndicate acquiring a cast-iron monopoly over the supply and circulation of the money not just of England, but of the whole world...

OMNIA VERITAS

Discover the Secret behind the Muslim Brotherhood, the globalist's tool for world dominion.

Omnia Veritas Ltd presents :

THE Globalists & Islamists

Fomenting the "Clash of Civilizations" for a New World Order

Who is pulling the string of Radical Islam ?

You will find out reading this astonishing work of Peter Goodgame!

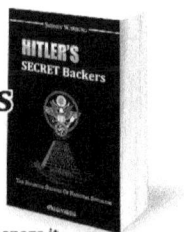

Omnia Veritas Ltd presents:

SANE SEX LIFE and SANE SEX LIVING

The time has come for a **book** like this to command the attention of **medical men...**

... they never learned sex. They never realized its fundamentals...

Omnia Veritas Ltd presents:

Monarchy or Money POWER *by* **ROBERT MCNAIR WILSON**

The meaning of Monarchy's struggle against the Money Power

A **master-piece** of history

The true nature of Kingship revealed!

Omnia Veritas Ltd presents:

The BabylonianWoe *by* **DAVID ASTLE**

"There was a class of persons who very well understood each other's interests, who very likely were related by racial and religious custom, and whose supra-nationalism transcended all city boundaries and borders of states."

"Yesterday it was a *conspiracy against the men of a city*, or a relatively small state; today a *conspiracy against the whole world*."

David Astle's masterpiece in a brand new edition!

www.ingramcontent.com/pod-product-compliance
Lightning Source LLC
Chambersburg PA
CBHW070258290326
41930CB00041B/2643